Dukan Diet Friendly Recip
For British Tastes With Food
Available In UK Shops And
Supermarkets

By Michelle Newbold
© Budding Books 2013

reading this book and did not purchase it, or it was not purchased for your use only, then please purchase your own copy.   Thank you for respecting the hard work of this author.

Contents:

Introduction:

A French doctor, Dr. Pierre Dukan, MD, devised the Dukan Diet and is one of the most popular diets followed in France and across the world today.

About 12 years ago, Dr Dukan introduced his eating plan, and it proved so popular that it quickly spread across the world, and is now quoted as one of the world top ten popular diets alongside the Atkins Diet, South Beach Diet, and the Mediterranean Diet.

Like most of the other popular diets, it progresses through stages eliminating certain food groups for a period of time, and gradually reintroducing them back into your everyday diet.

Once you have progressed through all the phases of the diet, you should be in a position to be able to eat pretty much anything you like for the rest of your life.

Many celebrities claim to have had great success following the Dukan diet, and probably the most famous of these, Kate Middleton, is said to have used the diet before her marriage to Prince William.

The diet starts off with the attack phase; where for around 5 to 10 days you are basically restricted to eating lean meats, eggs, fish and low fat dairy products. Eating these high protein foods mean your body burns a lot of calories while they are being digested, so in effect you are using more calories to burn these foods than they are worth. However all these delicious foods pack a fantastic nutritional punch, so you will not be depriving your body of any nutrients while working your way through this stage.

The following stage is called the cruise phase. This is where you are allowed to add in more foods, namely non-starchy vegetables. As your body can break down vegetables relatively easily, they will require less calories to burn, but as vegetables are low in calories anyway, the end result will be a pretty even balance between calories taken in and calories burned during digestion. During this stage you alternate one protein and vegetable eating day with one pure protein 'attack phase' day.

Your weight loss will slow during the cruise phase, but this is good because it gives your body a chance to adjust to your new way of eating, and allows your skin to tighten up to avoid sagginess usually associated with fast weight loss.

It is advised for you to stay on the cruise phase until you have reached your desired weight, or you are at a weight you feel comfortable living with.

When you move onto the third stage, or the consolidation phase as it is called, a wider range of food becomes available to you. Although some of these foods will pack a calorific punch, your new faster metabolism should be able to handle these relatively well without too much risk of weight gain.

Some fresh fruits are re-introduced at this phase, as well as wholegrain bread and a couple of servings of pasta and potatoes per week, although you are still advised to limit the quantities of starchy foods to small portions.

By the time you have progressed to the fourth phase, called the stabilization phase, your body should have adapted to eating just about any food without a problem, and you should have trained your taste buds to prefer the flavour of lean meats, fish, eggs, and vegetables over those more rich foods with denser calorie counts.

However, during this final stage you are required to stick to one day per week of eating only lean meats, fish and eggs, which is not an unrealistic habit to maintain. Doing this will also keep your metabolism running at its optimum level, so that it can easily cope with more calorific food consumed during the week to follow.

Gentle exercise is positively encouraged throughout all the diet phases, so if you can start with something as simple as a 15 minute walk per day while following the attack phase, then gradually build up the duration of your walks as your fitness levels improve. You will find it much easier to move and exercise after your initial weight loss, so try introducing new activities or take up a sport when you feel able to. You will burn off body fat much quicker when you combine this diet with regular aerobic exercise.

Following this diet has proven successful for countless people over the past decade, however there is a risk of you becoming bored of your restricted food choices, especially during the first stage where you are limited to lean meats, fish, eggs and low fat dairy.

To combat boredom you must arm yourself with a selection of tasty, quick to prepare dishes to help keep you going through each phase of the diet. This book gives you a nice range of simple to prepare, yet very tasty recipes to get you through each stage with ease.

So join with me and enjoy this collection of Dukan diet friendly recipes, watch the weight melt away while you enjoy flavourful meals, and never feel deprived, or like you are following a restrictive diet.

What You Can Drink On The Dukan Diet

Drinking plenty of fluids throughout the day is a very important part of the Dukan diet, especially during your protein only days. Dr Dukan suggests 2-3 litres of liquids per day, and to most dieters starting out it can seem like a difficult task, but it is not as scary as you may think, and keeping yourself hydrated will also help to avoid sugar cravings along the way.

People often think they feel hungry when in reality they can be dehydrated, and a refreshing drink will often cure false hunger pangs, and help you through to your next meal.

Don't believe you can only drink water on this diet. This is far from the truth, and when you take into consideration you can still drink tea and coffee, which sometimes are banned from other diets, it doesn't seem like such a hard target to reach.

The diet encourages you to take a drink with every meal you have, and you can choose from the following drinks:

Bottled, sparkling, or tap water
Tea without sugar, but you are allowed sweeteners and skimmed milk
Early Grey, Assam, Darjeeling etc.
Herbal tea
Coffee without sugar, but you are allowed sweeteners and skimmed milk
Diet drinks such as diet Pepsi, coke zero, sugar free squash, and any other sugar-free drink.

Note: made sure these drinks are not labelled as 'no sugar added'. This means there could be naturally occurring sugars in the drink, such as fruit juice, and therefore not suitable for this diet.

Phase One: The Attack Phase Friendly Recipes

The diet starts off with the attack phase; where for around 5 to 10 days you are basically restricted to eating lean meats, eggs, fish and low fat dairy products. Eating these high protein foods mean your body burns a lot of calories while they are being digested, so in effect you are using more calories to burn these foods than they are worth. However all these delicious foods pack a fantastic nutritional punch, so you will not be depriving your body of any nutrients while working your way through this stage.

Attack Phase Breakfasts Foods

Breakfast is often the most difficult meal to prepare on any diet, but with the Dukan diet the choice of these high-protein foods can make breakfast much easier. It is also very important to drink plenty of water during all stages of the Dukan diet, so try to aim for at least 6 glasses of water per day, as well as any tea or coffee you may also consume.

Here is a list of suggested food choices for breakfast that you can mix and match to suit your particular tastes.

Low fat yoghurt
Cottage cheese
Scrambled eggs
Soft-boiled eggs
Poached eggs
Omelette
Lean ham slices

Lean turkey slices
Lean chicken slices
Lean roast beef slices
Low fat cream cheese
Frozen prawns (defrosted)
Poached haddock
Skimmed milk
Oat bran (1 ½ tablespoons allowed per day only)
Tea and coffee
Artificial sweetener

Some example breakfast combinations follow.

Oat Bran Porridge

Serves 1:
1 ½ tablespoons of oat bran
100 – 150ml skimmed milk
1 teaspoon vanilla extract
Sweetener to taste (optional)

Combine the oat bran in a microwave proof bowl
with the milk, vanilla extract and sweetener if using.
Microwave on high for 1 minute, stir well and let
stand for a further 1 minute. Microwave for 30
seconds to heat through, stir and serve.

Yoghurt With Oat Bran

Serves 1:
1 pot of low fat yoghurt of your choice.
½ tablespoon oat bran
1 small pinch of cinnamon

Mix the yoghurt with the oat bran and leave to stand

in the fridge overnight. Sprinkle over a pinch of
cinnamon just before serving.

Cottage Cheese Roll-Ups

Serves 1:
3 tablespoons low fat cottage cheese
1 tablespoon low fat cream cheese
3 slices of lean turkey or ham
Salt and pepper to taste

Mix together the cottage cheese and cream cheese
in a bowl. Season with a little salt and pepper.
Divide the cheese mixture evenly between the slices
of meat and spread over the surface of each slice.
Roll up each slice of meat and eat.

Smoked Haddock Omelette

Serves 2:
275g/10oz smoked haddock fillet
3 bay leaves
300ml/10fl oz water
300ml/10floz skimmed milk
6 black peppercorns
6 eggs
Salt and pepper

Mix the water and milk together in a saucepan and
bring to the boil.

Add the bay leaves, peppercorns, and smoked
haddock and poach the fish for about 3-4 minutes,
until the fish is cooked and flakes easily with a fork.

Lift out the fish onto a plate and leave until cool, then using a fork break into flakes, remove any skin and bones and discard.

Heat the grill to hot. Whisk the eggs together with some salt and pepper.
Heat a large frying pan over a medium heat, and add a little olive oil or low fat cooking spray.

Pour in the eggs and stir gently until they start to set, shake the pan to evenly distribute the runny egg and lift the edges of the omelette with a spatula to allow the uncooked egg to run underneath.
When the omelette is set underneath but still runny on top, sprinkle over the flaked smoked haddock.

Put the omelette under the hot grill until the top has just set.

Chilli Prawns And Smoked Salmon With Scrambled Eggs

Serves 1:
½ garlic clove, chopped
1 medium egg, scrambled
1 tsp horseradish sauce
100g/3½oz smoked salmon
150g/5oz fresh or frozen prawns, defrosted
Juice of ½ a lemon
Pinch dried chilli flakes

Heat a frying pan over a medium heat. Add the prawns, smoked salmon, chilli flakes and garlic and fry gently for two minutes stirring regularly.

Place the lemon juice and horseradish sauce into a bowl and mix well.

Add the prawns and smoked salmon to the dressing and stir gently to coat.

Serve on a warm plate with the scrambled egg.

Simple Poached Eggs

Serves 2
1 tbsp white wine vinegar
2 eggs
Salt and pepper

Fill a small pan just over one third full with boiling water.
Add the vinegar and turn on the heat to simmering point.

Crack the eggs one at a time into a small bowl to check they are not bad, and then gently tip each egg into the simmering water.

Lightly poach for 3-4 minutes.

Remove with a slotted spoon and transfer to a warm plate.

Season with salt and pepper and serve immediately.

Baked Eggs In Ham Cups

Serves 2
4 medium eggs
4 tablespoons low fat/no fat cream cheese or crème fraiche
4 thin ham slices

Fit one slice of ham into each cup of a muffin tray, or a Yorkshire pudding tray.

The ham will stick up over the edges, but that's fine. Add one tablespoon of cream cheese or crème fraiche to each cup. Sprinkle with salt and pepper to taste.

Break an egg into each ham cup, and place the tray into an oven heated to 400F / 200C / Gas 6, for around 15 minutes until the egg whites have set, but the yolk is still runny.

Lift from the trays carefully using two spoons and serve on a warm plate.

Attack Phase Lunch Foods

During the attack phase you will rely on protein foods for every meal, regardless of whether it is breakfast, lunch, or dinner, and for between-meal snacks too.

Any of the foods and recipes mentioned in the breakfast section can also be eaten for lunch or dinner if it fits well with your own routine – especially those that use ready prepared ingredients and are served cold, such as the cottage cheese roll-ups, if you have to take your lunch to work with you.

Here are some suggested lunch foods, and some recipes that can be made to eat at home, or made ahead of time to carry with you to work, or if you are going out for the day.

Cold cuts of roast beef, chicken, ham, and turkey. Cooked chicken pieces

Chicken drumsticks
Crabsticks
Smoked mackerel
Cottage cheese
Low fat cheese triangles (Laughing Cow etc.)
Tinned tuna in spring water
Tinned salmon
Cold hardboiled eggs
Scotch eggs (recipe later)
Crustless Quiche (recipe later)
Skinless chicken breasts
Salmon steaks
Lean beefsteak, cubed

One stumbling block often experienced on the Dukan diet is ensuring you eat the recommended amount of oat bran each day. Dr Dukan recommends that people on the attack phase eat 1½ tablespoons of oat bran per day, and most dieters feel comfortable eating this at breakfast time. However, to avoid the possible boredom of facing oat bran for breakfast every day, you may choose to eat it at lunch or dinner.

Try this delicious oat bran pancake recipe as a quick lunch. It can be eaten as it is straight from the frying pan, or leave to cool and spread a little cream cheese inside, and roll up to make a tasty packed lunch to take to work with you.

Cinnamon Oat Bran Pancake

Serves 1
1 1/2 tablespoons oat bran

1 egg, beaten
1/2 teaspoon ground cinnamon
2 tablespoons low fat vanilla yoghurt
Sweetener to taste (optional)

Beat the egg and whisk in the vanilla yoghurt.

Stir in the cinnamon, oat bran, and sweetener (if using).

Use a little spray oil in a frying pan and pour the mixture in and cook for a couple of minutes on each side until brown.

For variety, you can substitute the ground cinnamon for another sweet spice such as ginger, or ground mixed spice blend.

A selection of recipes for attack phase lunches. Scale the recipes up or down to suit the number of people who are eating.

Home Made Scotch Eggs

Makes 6 Scotch Eggs
1 egg, beaten
2 tsp mixed dried herbs
500 gm lean mince
6 hard-boiled eggs
Oat bran
Salt and ground pepper

Mix the mince with the beaten egg in a bowl with the seasoning and herbs.

Divide into 6 equal portions, mould each portion around a hard-boiled egg to cover completely.

Sprinkle some oat bran onto a plate and roll the scotch eggs in the oat bran to lightly cover.

Place the scotch eggs on a baking tray and bake in the oven at 200C for around 30 minutes or until juices run clear.

Serve hot, or cold.

Asian Style Baked Salmon Steak

Serves 2
 1 red chilli, chopped
2 tbsp chopped fresh chives
2 tbsp chopped fresh coriander
2 tbsp chopped fresh root ginger
2 tbsp soy sauce
1 onion, chopped
200g/7oz salmon steak
Salt and pepper

Heat the oven to 200C/400F/Gas 6.

Take a sheet of foil large enough to wrap the salmon steak in to make a parcel.

 Place the salmon in the centre of the foil. Scatter over the chopped ginger, onion, chilli and herbs, drizzle over the soy sauce and season with salt and pepper.

Bring the sides of the foil up and crimp together to create a sealed parcel. The salmon will steam in this parcel and all the flavours from the extra ingredients will infuse the flesh.

Place the salmon parcel onto a baking tray, and cook in the oven for 15 minutes, or until the salmon is cooked through.

Remove the salmon from the parcel, and place onto a warm plate. Drizzle over some of the cooking juices from the foil and serve.

Cheesy Turkey Burgers

Serves 1
1 egg, beaten
1 tbsp chopped fresh thyme
250g/9oz turkey mince
50g/2oz low or zero fat cream cheese
Salt and pepper

Heat the oven to 200C/400F/Gas 6, and warm the grill to medium.

Place the mince, thyme, egg and salt and pepper into a bowl and mix together well.

Divide the turkey mixture into two and form each into a ball.
Push your thumb into the centre of each ball to form a hollow and stuff each with the cream cheese, then seal the mince to cover the cheese and seal it back up. Gently flatten into a burger shape.

Put the burgers under the grill on a medium heat and grill for two minutes on each side, until evenly browned, then transfer to the oven to cook for a further ten minutes, or until cooked through and the meat juices run clear.

Crustless Quiche

This is one of my favourite recipes, and is really handy as you can adapt it to use up whatever leftover meats you have that need using up!

Making a crustless quiche is just like making a regular quiche, but without the pastry, so it becomes a really quick and easy dish to throw together in a hurry and can be eaten hot or cold.

I like lots of tasty meats in quiche, so I will always throw in a decent handful of chopped cooked ham along with whatever else I can find. You can also use this recipe on the other phases of the Dukan diet, and include finely diced cooked vegetables and low fat cheese.

To make one large 9 inch dish:
1 garlic clove, crushed
1 onion, finely sliced
1 tsp chilli flakes
1 tsp dried mixed herbs
200g/7oz cooked ham, chopped
200g/7oz cooked meats of your choice, chopped
200ml/7fl oz skimmed milk
3 eggs
pinch nutmeg
Salt and pepper

Heat the oven to 150C/300F/Gas 2.

Spray a little cooking oil into a frying pan and gently fry the onion and garlic until soft.

Transfer the onion mixture to a deep pie dish and

spread well to cover the base.

Combine the eggs, milk, nutmeg and other seasoning in a bowl and mix well.

Bake for 25-30 minutes, or until set. Remove from the oven and serve hot, or leave to cool completely and eat cold cut into slices.

Spiced Beef Kebabs

Serves 1
1 tsp ground mixed spice
200g/7oz beef fillet, chopped into bite-sized pieces
Cooking spray
fresh parsley
Granulated sweetener equivalent to 1 tbsp of sugar
lemon wedges
salt and pepper

For the kebabs, place the beef cubes into a mixing bowl and sprinkle with the sweetener, mixed spice and spray with a little cooking oil and mix to completely coat the beef.

Thread the beef pieces onto two skewers and season well with salt and pepper.

Heat a griddle pan or grill and cook the kebabs on a high heat for 4-5 minutes on each side turning frequently, or until cooked through.

To serve, place the kebabs onto a plate, top with

chopped fresh parsley, and garnish with lemon wedges.

Tandoori Chicken Drumsticks With Chilli Dip

Serves 4
1.75kg/4lbs chicken drumsticks (remove the skin)
3-4 tbsp ready made dried tandoori spice mix
500g/1lb 2oz plain yoghurt
juice of 2 lemons
pinch of salt and pepper

To prepare the dipping sauce
1 chilli, sliced (seeds removed)
3-4 tbsps natural yoghurt
A few sprigs of fresh mint
pinch of salt
pinch of sweetener

Cut slits into the chicken meat with a small, sharp knife. Place the chicken into a bowl and sprinkle over the salt, pepper and the lemon juice, rubbing into the chicken flesh until well coated.

Whisk the yoghurt and tandoori spice mix together in a bowl until well combined. Pour the yoghurt mix over the chicken and rub well into the flesh. Cover with cling film and leave to marinade in the fridge overnight.

Heat the grill to hot.

Lift out the drumsticks and gently shake off any excess marinade. Place a wire rack over a roasting tin and lay the drumsticks on top of it. Grill the drumsticks for 20 minutes, turning frequently, until the chicken is cooked through.

For the dip, place all of the dipping sauce ingredients into a food processor and blend until smooth. Serve with the drumsticks.

DON'T FORGET TO DRINK PLENTY OF WATER!

Phase Two: Cruise Phase Friendly Recipes

The cruise phase is where you are allowed to add in more foods, namely non-starchy vegetables. As your body can break down vegetables relatively easily, they will require less calories to burn, but as vegetables you are allowed are low in calories anyway, the end result will be a pretty even balance between calories taken in and calories burned during digestion. During this stage you alternate one protein and vegetable eating day with one pure protein 'attack phase' day.

Your weight loss will slow during the cruise phase, but this is good because it gives your body a chance to adjust to your new way of eating, and allows your skin to tighten up to avoid the sagginess usually associated with fast weight loss.

It is advised for you to stay on the cruise phase until you have reached your desired weight, or you are at a weight you feel comfortable living with.

You are also advised to increase your daily allowance of oat bran from 1½ tablespoons per day to 2 tablespoons per day. You can adjust any of the oat bran recipes found in the attack phase to incorporate the extra half a tablespoon.

Here is a list of low starch vegetables that are allowed on this phase of the diet.

Foods that can be added to your diet every other day are:

Asparagus
Aubergine
Broccoli
Cabbage
Cauliflower
Celery
Courgette
Cucumber
Fennel
Green beans
Leeks
Mushrooms
Onions
Peppers
Radish
Spinach
Salad leaves
Tomatoes

Occasionally you are also allowed to eat carrots, beetroot and artichokes, but these more starchy vegetables should be consumed in small portions no more than twice per week.

You can add a portion of vegetables from the allowed list to your meals as a side dish to be eaten as they are, or incorporate them into a recipe to add variety and extra flavour to your dishes. Examples would be beef and spinach soup, ham and mushroom crust-less quiche, and steamed chicken with leeks and mushrooms.

Banned foods during the cruise phase: You are not allowed to eat these foods during this phase because of the higher starch content these foods contain:

Any fruit
Avocado
Beans
Lentils
Peas
Potatoes
Sweetcorn

Try these tasty recipes:

Chicken With Leeks And Mushrooms

Serves 2
1 leek, diced finely
1 shallot, finely chopped
100g/4oz mushrooms, sliced
2 skinless chicken breasts
2 sprigs tarragon
2 tbsp fresh parsley, chopped
50ml/2fl oz low fat fromage frais
A little cooking spray
A pinch of curry powder
A pinch of turmeric
Salt and pepper

Steam the chicken breasts and tarragon for 10-15 minutes until cooked through and no signs of pink.

In a lidded saucepan, spray a little cooking spray to prevent sticking and sweat the shallots, leeks and mushrooms with the curry powder and turmeric over a medium-low heat until softened but not brown.

Add the parsley and fromage frais, bring to the boil and simmer very gently for a few minutes. Season with salt and pepper and serve with the steamed chicken breasts.

Beef And Spinach Soup

Serves 2
225g/1/2lb fresh spinach
90g/3oz lean fillet steak, very thinly sliced

For the marinade
1 shallot, finely sliced
1 tbsp finely chopped garlic
1/2 tbsp Worcestershire sauce
Pepper

For the soup
1 tbsp lemon juice
1 small, fresh red chilli, seeded and chopped
1/2 litre/1 pint chicken stock
1/2 tbsp Worcestershire sauce
1/2 tsp sweetener

Remove the stalks from the spinach and wash the leaves well to remove any dirt.
Blanch the leaves for a few seconds in boiling water, drain well and refresh in cold water to prevent further cooking. Drain well, squeezing out any excess water with your hands.

Combine the steak with the shallot, garlic, one tablespoon of Worcestershire sauce and a pinch of pepper. Leave to marinate until you are ready to cook.

Bring the chicken stock to a simmer in a large saucepan and season it with Worcestershire sauce, the lemon juice, sweetener and chilli.

Add the blanched spinach and stir in the beef and all of the marinade from the bowl. Bring the soup to a simmering point, and simmer for just a couple of minutes. Check for seasoning and add more pepper if needed. Serve at once.

Stuffed Turkey Breast

Serves 2
2 garlic cloves, crushed
2 tablespoons low fat cream cheese
2 turkey breast fillets
6 slices thin sandwich ham
A little cooking spray
A small handful of fresh mint, chopped
Salt and pepper

Heat the oven to 200C/400F/Gas 6.

Blend the ham slices, one of the turkey fillets, garlic, mint and seasoning in a food processor until smooth.

Place the remaining turkey breast between two sheets of cling film, and using a rolling pin, carefully bash the fillet until its about 1/2 inch thick to make an escalope.

Spread the stuffing over the flattened-out breast and roll up. Season the breast with salt and pepper.

Spray a frying pan with a little cooking spray and fry the roll for three minutes on each side until lightly browned all over.
Transfer the roll to a baking dish and bake in the oven until cooked through and any meat juices run clear.

Once cooked, remove from the oven and place on a chopping board. Cut into thick slices and serve with vegetables of your choice from the allowed list.

Smoked Salmon and Fennel Salad

Serves 1
½ fennel bulb, very finely sliced
1 tsp olive oil
100g/3½oz thin slices of smoked salmon
Juice and jest of 1 lime
Salt and pepper

Zest the lime, and squeeze the juice into a bowl.
Add the olive oil, and whisk together. Add the
fennel to the bow, stir to coat the leaves and leave to
marinate for a few minutes.

To serve, place the fennel salad onto a plate, top
with the sliced smoked salmon and season with salt
and pepper.

Vegetable Omelette

Serves 1
1 red chilli, deseeded and diced
1 small aubergine, cut into small chunks
1 tbsp soy sauce
75g/2¾oz tofu, cut into small cubes
A little cooking spray
Juice of 1 lime

For the omelette
1 tbsp soy sauce

3 eggs
50ml/2fl oz skimmed milk
A little cooking spray

Spray a little cooking spray to coat a hot frying pan or wok, and add the aubergine and chilli. Stir-fry for about 3 minutes then add the tofu, soy sauce and limejuice. Quickly stir fry for about a minute stirring continuously until the tofu is heated through and well coated. Take off the heat and leave to one side while you prepare the omelette.

For the omelette, in a large mixing bowl beat the eggs with the milk and soy sauce.
Spray a medium-sized frying pan with a little cooking spray, and place the egg mixture into the pan and cook for two minutes over a medium heat.

Spoon the cooked vegetables over one half of the omelette, then fold over the other half.
Cook for about a minute to heat everything through and serve hot.

Garlic Prawns

Serves 3
½ onion, finely chopped
1 chilli, deseeded, chopped
1/2 tbsp paprika
150g/6oz cooked, frozen peeled prawns, defrosted
2 garlic cloves, chopped
A little cooking spray

Heat a frying pan sprayed with a little cooking spray, add the garlic, chillies, paprika and onion. Cook until the onion is soft and translucent, but not browned.

Add the prawns to the frying pan, and increase the heat a little. Cook for 5-10 minutes stirring regularly.

Serve hot.

Chicken with Green Beans and Tomato

Serves 2
1 200g tin of chopped tomatoes
1 clove of garlic, chopped
1 spring onion, chopped
2 skinless, boneless chicken breasts, cubed
200g/1/2lb frozen green beans, thawed
A little cooking spray
A small handful chopped fresh basil
Salt and pepper

Heat a large frying pan over medium hot heat and spray with a little cooking oil.
Add the garlic and spring onion and sauté gently for 2 minutes, then add the chicken cubes and cook through until no longer pink.

Stir in the tinned tomatoes and chopped basil, season well with salt and pepper, and bring to a gentle boil. Reduce the heat and simmer for 10 minutes stirring occasionally.

Serve hot. This dish also freezes well.

Vary your salad ingredients to keep meals interesting.

Phase Three: Consolidation Phase

Dr Dukan advises you stay on this phase of the diet for 5 days for every pound of weight you have lost. So for example if you lost 10lb in weight following the attack and cruise phase, you should stay on the consolidation phase for 50 days (10 x 5 = 50).

The consolidation phase offers a wider range of food to you. Although some of these foods will pack a calorific punch, your new faster metabolism should be able to handle these relatively well without too much risk of weight gain.

Some fresh fruits are re-introduced at this phase, as well as wholegrain bread and a couple of servings of pasta and potatoes per week, although you are still advised to limit the quantities of starchy foods to small portions.

Your daily oat bran intake remains the same as it was at the cruise phase at two tablespoons per day, but with the reintroduction of some fruits, you will have more ways of combining your oat bran in interesting and tasty recipes.

You can now add 2 slices of wholemeal bread every day, which may make lunchtimes easier if you like to pack a sandwich for lunch at work, or really missed eating your morning toast. You can use low fat spread on your bread, but make sure it is just a thin scrape rather than a generous slather.

Also allowed at this stage are some cheeses. So if you are partial to a bit of cheese on toast, or a cheese sandwich for lunch, then you can enjoy these treats again. However, try not to eat more than 40g of cheese per day, and not all cheeses are acceptable on the diet.

Steer clear of these cheeses: Brie, Camembert, goat's cheese and blue cheese.

If you are a meat lover, this is the phase of the diet where you can once again enjoy lean cuts of pork and lamb. These are more fatty meats, so try not to over-indulge too often, and instead stick to leaner meats for most days of the week maybe saving pork and lamb for the weekend, or special meals.

Other more starchy foods are reintroduced on the consolidation phase including rice, pasta, beans and lentils. However, it is advised to only have one portion of these starchy foods per week, and stick to eating no more than a 225g serving. Choose brown rice over white rice, and whole-wheat pasta over white pasta.

Potatoes can also be eaten in moderation at this stage, but cook them without fat, and eat them with their skins as the fibre contained in the skins will slow down the impact of the carbs on your blood sugar levels.

Fruits allowed on the consolidation phase:
Apples
Berries (strawberries, raspberries etc.)
Grapefruit

Kiwi fruit
Mangoes
Melon
Nectarines
Oranges
Peaches
Pears
Plums

Fruits not allowed on the consolidation phase:
Bananas
Cherries
Dried fruit (raisins, currants, sultanas etc.)
Grapes

Consolidation Phase Friendly Recipes

Turkey Lasagne

Serves 4
1 carrot, peeled and finely chopped
1 clove garlic, crushed
1 green pepper, seeded and finely chopped
1 large ripe tomato
1 onion, peeled and chopped
1 tbsp mixed dried herbs
125g/4oz lean smoked back bacon, chopped
150g Wholemeal lasagne sheets
150ml/5fl oz chicken stock
160g low fat mozzarella cheese, sliced
2 teaspoons olive oil
225g/8oz lean minced turkey
400g/14oz tinned tomatoes
Salt and pepper

Heat a frying pan and add the mince. Cook over a high heat until cooked and no pink bits remain, and drain off any fat.

Heat the olive oil in another pan over a medium heat and cook the onion, carrot and green pepper until they start to soften, but don't let them brown.

Stir in the crushed garlic, chopped bacon and the dried herbs and cook for 2 minutes, stirring well to combine.

Tip in the tinned tomatoes and the stock and season well with salt and pepper.

Add the cooked mince to the pan, bring to a boil, turn down the heat and simmer gently for 40-50 minutes, stirring occasionally.

Heat the oven to 190C/375F/Gas 5

Spoon a layer of meat sauce over the base of a large baking dish.
Lay half the lasagne sheets over the meat, and repeat the layers until all the meat and lasagne sheets have been used up finishing with a layer of meat on top.

Slice the ripe tomato into thin slices and lay these over the top of the lasagne alternating with slices of mozzarella cheese.

Cover with foil and bake for 35-40 minutes until the lasagne sheets are soft. Remove the foil and bake for another five minutes just to brown the top.

Serve hot.

Beef Stir-Fry with Egg Fried rice

Serves 2
Egg fried rice ingredients:
2 eggs
2 tbsp soy sauce
200g/7oz cooked brown rice

Stir-fry ingredients:

½ onion, thinly sliced
1 courgette, thinly sliced
1 red pepper, thinly sliced
2 garlic clove, crushed
2 tbsp sesame oil
2 tbsp sesame seeds
2 tbsp soy sauce
2 tbsp sweetener
200g/7oz lean beef, sliced into thin strips
Salt and pepper

To make the egg fried rice - place a large frying pan
or wok over a high heat.

Tip the cooked brown rice and soy sauce into a
large mixing bowl and mix together until all the rice
is well coated. Add the rice to the frying pan or wok
and keep stirring for one minute.

Crack the eggs into the rice and stir for a minute
until the eggs have cooked.
Spoon the egg fried rice into a warm bowl, put into
the oven on a low heat to keep warm while you
prepare the stir-fry.

For the stir-fry, place the soy sauce, sweetener, and
sesame oil into a large bowl, and add the sliced beef
to the mixture and leave to marinate for five
minutes.

Heat your frying pan or wok to a hot heat and add in
the courgette, red pepper, onion, garlic, marinated
beef and sesame seeds and stir-fry for two minutes
keeping the food moving to ensure even cooking.

Tip in any of the marinade juices left from the beef

and cook for a further 2 or 3 minutes. Season, to taste, with salt and pepper.

Serve hot over the egg fried rice.

Light Chicken Salad with Fresh Nectarines

Serves: 4
1/2 red onion, thinly sliced
120ml low fat salad dressing of your choice
2 large fresh nectarines, sliced
280g leftover cooked chicken
350g spinach leaves or mixed salad greens
60g toasted sesame seeds

Place nectarine slices, chicken and red onion in a large mixing bowl, toss with just enough dressing to coat. (You can vary the flavour of the salad by trying different salad dressings, but check the labels to make sure they are low in fat and sugar). Add spinach leaves and sesame seeds and toss to coat. Mound salad on large plate and season with salt and pepper.

Crispy Apple Salad

Serves: 2
1 shallots, finely sliced
1 Granny Smith apple, cored and sliced
1 sweet eating apple, cored and sliced
3 cherry tomato's, cut into quarters
1 tbsp toasted sesame seeds

Fresh coriander leaves, chopped
1 garlic clove, finely chopped
1 tsp sweetener
1 tbsp fish sauce
Juice of 1 fresh lime
1/2 tbsp vegetable oil
1/2 tbsp limejuice
1/2 red chilli, finely chopped (seeds removed)

Make the dressing by blending together the garlic, chilli and sweetener in a food processor to make a paste. Add the fish sauce and limejuice and season to taste with a little salt and pepper.

For the salad, fry the shallots in the oil for around 5 minutes or until crisp and golden brown. Drain on kitchen paper.

Toss the sliced apples in the limejuice, and mix with the tomatoes and dressing.

Serve topped with the sesame seeds, shallots and chopped coriander. This goes well with lean cold cuts of ham or pork.

Apple Oat Bran Muffins

Serves 6
1 Tbsp Sugar Free Vanilla Pudding Powder
1 tsp baking powder
1 tsp Cinnamon
2 Eggs
2 Tbsp Sweetener
6 Tbsp Fat Free Apple Turnover Yoghurt

8 Tbsp Oat Bran

Mix all the dry ingredients together and whisk in the egg, vanilla and yoghurt.

Spray a non stick muffin tray with a little cooking spray, divide the batter evenly between 6 of the holes, and cook at 350 degrees /180 C / Gas 4 for 15-18 minutes until lightly brown and cooked through.

Cool on a wire rack. Seal in an airtight container and store in the fridge.

Makes 6 average sized Muffins

Melon Berry Oat bran Smoothie

Serves 2
1/2 a punnet fresh raspberries
1/2 cantaloupe melon - peeled, seeded and cubed
100g (4 oz) low fat natural yoghurt
2 tablespoons oat bran

2 tablespoons sweetener

Combine the cantaloupe, yoghurt, raspberries, oat bran and sweetener. Add to a food processor and blend until smooth.

Add some crushed ice if you would like the drink chilled.

Pour into 2 large drinking glasses and serve.

Mango Fool

Serves 4
1 large mango
1-2 tablespoons sweetener
200g low fat fromage frais

Slice the mango in half and remove the flesh from the stone.
Blend half of the mango into a puree.

Place the mango puree in a large mixing bowl. Add the fromage frais and sweetener and carefully fold together, but don't overdo it, you want to have orange swirls running through the mixture.

Dice the remaining mango into small pieces. Spoon alternate layers of the fromage frais mixture and mango pieces into a large glass trifle bowl finishing with a layer of mango pieces.

Cover the bowl with cling film and chill until you are ready to serve.

Phase Four: Stabilization Phase

By the time you have progressed to the fourth and final phase of the diet, called the stabilization phase, your body should have adapted to eating just about any food without a problem, and you should have trained your taste buds to prefer the flavour of lean meats, fish, eggs, and vegetables over those more rich foods with denser calorie counts.

However, during this final stage you are required to stick to one day per week of eating only lean meats, fish and eggs, which is not an unrealistic habit to maintain. Doing this will also keep your metabolism running at its optimum level, so that it can easily cope with more calorific food consumed during the week to follow.

Use the protein only recipes from the Attack Phase of this book on your one protein day each week, or if you don't have time to cook a meal, make sure your fridge is stocked with some tasty protein rich foods to snack on during the day.

Dr Dukan strongly suggests that you choose a Thursday each week as your protein day, but if this is not a convenient day for you, then choose another day. But make sure you stick to the same day each week otherwise you risk jeopardising your weight loss.

If you decide one week to make Monday your protein only day, but the following week you choose Friday, you will be over feeding your body with carbohydrates for an extra 4 day without a break. This is a recipe for weight gain.

In the unfortunate event that you do gain a few unwanted pounds back despite your best efforts to stick to the diet, then try taking two protein only days per week instead of one. This way you are giving your body a rest from carbohydrates, and it helps give your metabolism a little boost. You should find that doing this helps you shake off the small weight gain and gets you back on track.

Always read food labels. If you are unsure if you are buying a product that is low fat or low sugar, then put it back. Watch out for hidden sugars in the food, you may be surprised by some of the names sugar is given by the food industry. Look out for ingredients like fructose, dextrose, barley malt, corn syrup, buttered syrup, cane crystals, corn sweetener, diastatic malt, ethyl maltol, sorbitol, galactose, lactose – anything that ends in ose is either a sugar or was derived from sugar. This is just a small sample, but there is thought to be around 70 different names used for sugar in food manufacturing.

If you are also sticking to the recommended level of regular exercise by this phase, you will be going a long way to keeping the lbs off. Don't worry if you are reading this section before starting the diet – don't worry, you don't have to turn yourself into some sort of exercise demon, or take up a competitive sport. Regular activity is the key to keeping the weight from creeping back on.

Try to work in some extra activity into your life by taking an evening stroll after dinner, or getting off the bus two stops early so you walk further. Take the stairs instead of the lift or the escalator. Leave the car at home and cycle or walk short journeys. Get yourself a dog – it will need walking regularly, and is great company for the family.

Remember these golden rules while following the Dukan Diet, and you should see great success with your weight loss and fitness levels:

Get your water quota in every day

It seems like a lot of water, but it does help to flush toxins from your system, keeps you hydrated, fills you up, and keeps false hunger pangs under control.

Don't let yourself get hungry

There is nothing worse than feeling hungry on a diet, and this is the surest way to make you fail.

Always have plenty of high protein snacks on hand to nibble on when you get the munchies.

Weigh yourself regularly to keep yourself motivated

If you are following the diet correctly you should see rapid weight loss very quickly in the beginning. Use the positive results to keep you going.

Plan to Cheat

There will be some days that you just have to give in to your cravings, or you are attending a social event with delicious diet-unfriendly food.

If you cheat sensibly it will not cause too much damage to your long-term weight loss goals. If you absolutely have to have chocolate for example, slowly eat a piece of 85% cocoa chocolate. You will satisfy your chocolate cravings without blowing your diet.

At the social event, work out which is the most high protein meal from the menu, and stick to eating that. Avoid the sweet trolley, and curb your appetite with lots of sparkling water before the meal.

Good luck with your diet. I hope it works for you as well as it has for the thousands of followers around the world.

Thank you for choosing this book, and I hope you enjoyed reading all the recipe ideas here. I hope you can find some favourite dishes that can help you with your weight-loss, and wish you and your family happiness and good health.

Printed in Great Britain
by Amazon.co.uk, Ltd.,
Marston Gate.